ARTHUR SLADE

Monsterology

*Fabulous Lives of
the Creepy, the Revolting,
and the Undead*

Illustrated by Derek Mah

Tundra Books

This book is dedicated to the monster under the bed.
Thanks for not eating me. – Arthur Slade

For Yook Lin Leong, who knows a little something
about monsters. – Derek Mah

Text copyright © 2005 by Arthur Slade
Illustrations copyright © 2005 by Derek Mah

Published in Canada by Tundra Books,
481 University Avenue, Toronto, Ontario M5G 2E9

Published in the United States by Tundra Books of Northern New York,
P.O. Box 1030, Plattsburgh, New York 12901

Library of Congress Control Number: 2004117245

Library and Archives Canada Cataloguing in Publication

Slade, Arthur G. (Arthur Gregory)
Monsterology : the fabulous lives of the creepy, the revolting, and the undead / Arthur Slade ; illustrated by Derek Mah.

ISBN 0-88776-714-1

1. Monsters–Juvenile fiction. 2. Children's stories, Canadian (English)
I. Mah, Derek II. Title.

PS8587.L343M66 2005   jC813'.54   C2004-907142-4

ONTARIO ARTS COUNCIL
CONSEIL DES ARTS DE L'ONTARIO

We acknowledge the financial support of the Government of Canada through the Book Publishing Industry Development Program (BPIDP) and that of the Government of Ontario through the Ontario Media Development Corporation's Ontario Book Initiative. We further acknowledge the support of the Canada Council for the Arts and the Ontario Arts Council for our publishing program.

Design: Kong Njo

Printed and bound in Canada

1 2 3 4 5 6   10 09 08 07 06 05

Contents

Monsterspotting Map	4
Dracula	6
Golem	12
Medusa	18
Loki	24
The Giant	30
Tera	36
Frankenstein's Monster	42
Sasquatch	48
Loch Ness Monster	54
Zack	60
Baba Yaga	66
Dr. Jekyll and Mr. Hyde	72
Quasimodo	78
Loba	84
The Grim Reaper	90

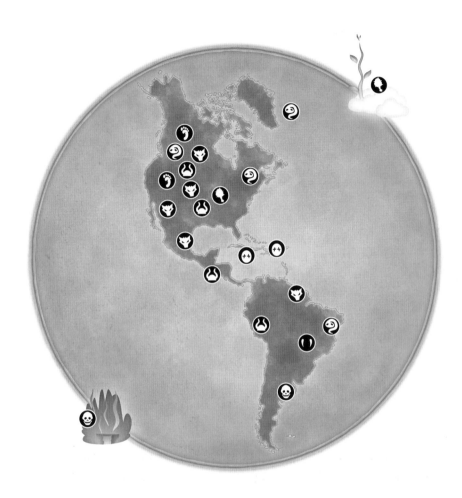

Monsters, monsters everywhere...

Think you're safe from monsters where you live?
Think again. Monsters lurk everywhere. There's probably
one under your bed right now — but don't look!
Just keep your feet tucked in.

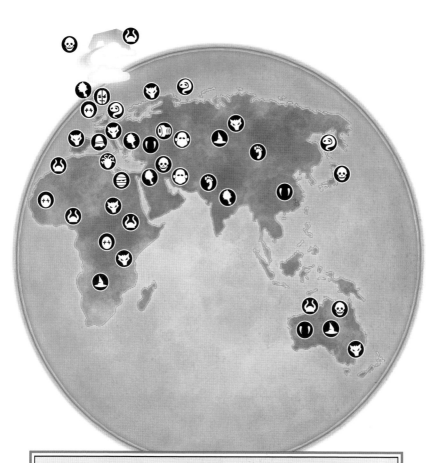

- 🝑 Vampire
- 🝑 Golem
- 🝑 Medusa
- 🝑 Trickster
- 🝑 Frankenstein's Monster
- 🝑 Giant
- 🝑 Mummy
- 🝑 Big Foot
- 🝑 Zombie
- 🝑 Sea Monster
- 🝑 Witch
- 🝑 Quasimodo
- 🝑 Werewolf
- 🝑 Grim Reaper
- 🝑 Dr. Jekyll and Mr. Hyde

Dracula

Age: Immortal

Loves: Blood types *A, O, B, AB*, also type *A* personalities, type *B* personalities, innocent teens, warm beating hearts

Hates: Tanning, surprise clerical visits, garlic pills, girls named Buffy, crucifixes

Fashion rating: *B+* Handsome and stylish, he's a walking, talking dream of an undead man. Unfortunately, he only dresses in one color: black.

Favorite saying: "I vant to suck your blood."

Favorite movies: *From Here to Eternity, Dracula, Nosferatu, Salem's Lot*

Favorite haunts: Dracula is drawn to castles, Victorian-style houses, and coffins layered with dirt from his homeland. He also likes to hang out at raves.

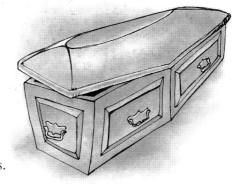

Transylvania mania: If you're planning a party, don't invite this nocturnal neck nibbler. Unless, of course, it's a Goth party. Dracula comes to us from tales of Vlad the Fourth, AKA Count Dracul – a Transylvanian nobleman who hung around in the 15th century. Vlad, a twisted Boy Scout type, earned his "bloodthirsty" badges by torturing his enemies – in fact he loved picnicking in a forest of prisoners impaled on wooden stakes. This is how he acquired the cute nickname "The Impaler." He spent his spare time luring innocent villagers into his creepy castle and dispatching them in whatever grisly manner he could imagine. In 1897, author Bram Stoker used Vlad and folktales of the *nosferatu* (undead) as inspiration to create the most famous fanged foe of all: Dracula.

Synopsis of sin, evil, death, and fine wine: *Dracula.* This is the book that puts the G in Gothic. It also puts the G in gross. Young and innocent, Jonathan Harker goes to Transylvania to help Count Dracula buy a house in England. While in the Count's castle, Harker is attacked by three vampiresses, sees Dracula crawling up the wall, is surrounded by wolves, and eventually imprisoned. He escapes, but by that time good ol' Drac has set up shop in London and is busy biting innocents. But Harker and a team of valiant vampire hunters relentlessly track him down and chase him back to Transylvania, where they finish him off. And he's gone forever. Until Hollywood starts making Dracula movies.

Cool fact: *Drakul* means "son of the dragon" and "devil" in Romanian.

Home: A castle near Borgo Pass, Transylvania

High-school memories: None. He had too much of a nightlife.

Shape-shifting charm: In person Dracula is charming, witty, and a great conversationalist, though his jokes are often from the 15th century. Just don't look too deeply into his eyes, as he has a mystical ability to hypnotize his victims. Next thing you know you'll wake up feeling drained. And don't arm wrestle with him, he has the strength of 20 men. He also has many other handy powers, including the ability to climb 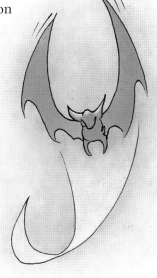 like an insect and transform into a wolf, a bat, or a greenish floating mist. It's a great party trick! He has fangs that extend to suck blood and retract whenever he needs to look innocent. Sadly, he has no reflection, therefore he doesn't know that his hairstyle hasn't changed in 500 years.

Interview with a vampire: "I'm just an honest undead man trying to make his way in the world; to find his place. I'm completely misunderstood. Is draining some pimply teens of all their blood really so bad? Is it? Now littering, that's something people should be worried about. Global warming! That's the real evil in the world. Not insignificant little vampires like me."

Invention he's been waiting an eternity for: A suntan lotion with a strong enough SPF for him to go outside.

The hunter and the huntee: If you find yourself pursued by Dracula just stop at the nearest Italian diner and smear yourself with garlic toast. Or go to a Chinese restaurant, grab a chopstick, and use a hard fortune cookie as a hammer – the best way to kill a vampire is to drive a wooden stake through its heart in one blow. You'd think that'd be enough, but no. Next you have the icky task of cutting off its head with a spade. Then you burn the parts and distribute the ashes to the wind. Just tell your parents you were having a wiener roast.

How to know if you're dating a vampire: If he asks you back to his coffin for coffee and a bite to eat, be suspicious.

How to tell if your teacher is a vampire: They're all vampires.

How to tell if your parents are vampires: Do they make you go to bed early? They're vampires.

Famous vampires: Dracula, Lestat, Vampirella, The Count, Count Chocula, Varney (Yep, there really was a vampire named Varney. People teased him about it, until he ripped their heads off, that is.)

Medical note: There is a theory that the bite of a vampire will cure acne. This is true. Unfortunately, you'll die before you get to enjoy the benefits.

Where Does a Blood-Sucking Fiend (BSF) Come From?

Vampires are definitely hip and very, very cool – cold in fact – mainly because their hearts don't beat and they have no blood. But how do warm-blooded, fun-loving human beings become BSFs? Well, first they die. At this point most people are kind enough to stay dead, but the occasional curmudgeon is so full of wickedness, sin, and cruelty that he rises from the grave with a pale complexion, bad hair, and a hunger for blood. He sees humans as fast food, and in order to live forever he must continually feed. Anyone who is bitten by a vampire and not completely drained of blood (and their life), will transform into a vampire. Vampires can appear in any country – Portugal, India, Ghana, Canada – though they prefer misty landscapes with large castles. Perhaps the most interesting vampire is the *Jiangshi*, or Chinese vampire, a mean, mean undead blood-sucking machine who hops at his victims, because the pain and stiffness of being dead prevents him from walking. You can stop him in his tracks by sticking a special charm on his forehead – remember it has to be written on a yellow piece of paper in chicken blood.

Golem

What he is: A magically created servant who does everything you tell him to do, no questions asked
What he isn't: Alive
Height: Seven feet
Personality type: He's the strong silent type. Really silent. He's mute.
Birthplace: Prague, Czech Republic
Fashion rating: D- He dresses as a sexton – that's a church officer who rings bells and digs graves. Ouch!
Loves: Doing the same task over and over again
Hates: When his master uses him as a stepladder
Occupation he'd most like to have if not a golem: Mime
Favorite movies: *The Golem, The Golem and the Dancer, The Golem: How He Came Into the World, Frankenstein*

Golem-making 101: The golem is perhaps the first and worst of all the monsters. Well, first anyway. Our tall, dark, and so handsome creature comes trudging out of Jewish legends. In the Middle Ages (those are the days between now and the Stone Age) very wise men learned how to use magic to turn a pile of clay into an automatic servant that could be commanded to do any mindless task (except homework). The most popular golem story took place in 1580 AD. Rabbi Löw lived in Prague where the Jews needed to be protected from Blood Libel (a made-up allegation that accused the Jews of killing Christian children to use their blood for making bread – now that's just plain gross). Some particularly nasty people even tried to plant dead bodies in the Jewish quarters to frame the Jews. Rabbi Löw asked heaven to help him, and lo and behold, he received the answer: Create a golem. So Löw and two assistants went to the River Moldau and sculpted a giant body out of clay by torchlight. They circled it seven times and recited a few special words until the clay glowed red and grew hair and nails. Then Rabbi Löw put a piece of parchment in the golem's mouth that had the real name of God written on it. After a few more recitations, the golem opened his eyes. They dressed him (can't have a naked golem slouching about) and took him to the synagogue. During the day the golem sat around not saying much (he was mute, as all golems are). At night the rabbi put an amulet on the golem that turned it invisible. The giant creature was then commanded to search the city for enemies – he'd find them, tie them up with rope, and leave them with the authorities (kind of like an early Batman). But as time passed, the golem became stronger and more forceful. In fact, he began killing the

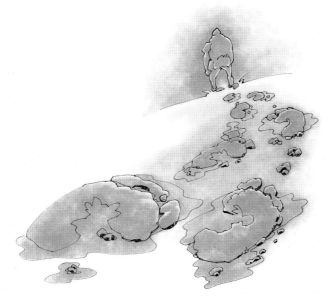

enemies and leaving their corpses lying around. People tend to get upset when you leave corpses around. When a law was finally passed to protect the Jews, Rabbi Löw decided to put a stop to the golem. He yanked out the piece of parchment from its mouth and the golem became a mass of clay. To this day the golem sits in the attic of his synagogue, waiting to be brought to life.

Interview with the golem: "So what's it like being a golem?"
Silence
"What's up? Whassup?"
Silence.
"So, like, you really are mute."
Silence.

Cool fact[1]: The golem has no soul. It has been given the *ruah*, which is "breath of bones" or "the life force." But it feels no pain and thinks no thoughts other than how to complete its task. It would be the perfect football player.

Cool fact[2]: In Hebrew golem means "shapeless mass."

Literally literal: Golems obey exact commands. One day Rabbi Löw's wife commanded the golem to fetch water and put it in her tub. Then she went out shopping. When she came home her whole house was flooded. Oops! She should have told him to stop once the tub was full.

1,001 great uses for golems: Carrying luggage, mowing the lawn, taking out the garbage, grad date, beating up the bullies who took your lunch money in grade five

A radically cool use for a golem: Command him to lie down. Place a piece of plywood over him and angle it toward a sidewalk. Then use him as a skateboard jump. Yahoo!

How to create your own golem: Another way to create a golem was to put together a clay man and write *emet* on its forehead, which is Hebrew for "truth." When you're done using the golem, just erase the first letter and you will have *met*, which means "death." He'll fall apart.

Holy homunculus! Throughout the centuries wise (and not so wise) men have sought to create golems. In the 16th century Paracelsus (his real name was Philippus Aureolus Theophrastus Bombastus von Hohenheim, but that's too long to put in this book) was a big, loud-mouthed Swiss physician who was brilliant and bombastic. If anyone dared to disagree with him, he called them "ignorant cabbages" and "sausage stuffers." Ouch! He had many groundbreaking theories about medicine, but his biggest boast was that he had created a homunculus – a replica of a human being that was 12 inches tall and did all sorts of chores. (Tie his shoes? Scratch his ankles?) "It's easy to make," he claimed. "Just get a bag of bones, skin fragments, and hair from any animal, and lay it on the ground surrounded by horse manure for 40 days. It will spontaneously grow from that." Wow, a 12-inch golem that smelled like horse poo. The guy was a genius!

The first golem: Perhaps the first golem was Enkidu, who appeared in a really old, old story called *The Epic of Gilgamesh*. Gilgamesh was this all powerful, snobby king who won every fight he was in. The gods created Enkidu, a wild man made of clay, who fought Gilgamesh to a standstill and almost beat him. They became great friends and had many adventures together.

High-school memories: Golem didn't go to school, but he did tear one down. That was before they had bulldozers.

Medusa

Age: Mid-20s

Height: Five foot four, or five foot eight, depending on whether her snakes are up or down

Hairstyle: Dreadlocks (though sometimes she calls them Deadlocks). Only she could wear a nest of snakes and pull it off.

Home: A palace on the edge of Lake Tritonis in Libya

Fashion rating: $A+$ Hissing snakes, a pouting look, beauty and death combined – Medusa makes any strutting waif look like a pretender. No woman is more avant-garde and stone-cold stunning!

Loves: Statues, hair that curls itself, turning her enemies to stone

Hates: Beheadings, when her snakes shed their skins, not being invited to parties

Favorite saying: "Just one look and you'll be hooked."

Abilities: Turns people to stone. Isn't that enough?

Romantic status: Single. Not by choice. No one will come near her.

Nicknames: Hissing Sista, Grim Face, Snake Eyes

From whence sprang Medusa: Whoa, first off, the Greek gods and goddesses were, like, completely ultra-weird, jealous, and petty. You'd think they were all going through puberty the way they acted. Medusa was an extremely dishy babe. Her beauty became so renowned that Medusa began to believe she was more gorgeous than Athena. Now, Athena was a hot goddess (I mean, like, a REAL goddess). She also had a bad temper. She dropped down out of the sky and transformed Medusa's to-die-for hair into snakes, and from that point on anyone who looked at her turned to stone. Medusa became, well, angry, fiery, spiteful, vengeful, and mopey. She turned all her enemies into stone and from then on lived in a palace with her two immortal sisters (they were known as the Gorgon sisters). The grounds were decorated, in a feng shui kinda way, with statues of men and beasts who had been turned to stone, including her lovers (who died dropping by to see her). Can you imagine how sad and frustrated she was? It was hard enough to get a date in ancient Greece without turning people to stone. Finally a hero named Perseus came to rescue her. Well, not really rescue. He had been ordered by the king to fetch her head. Athena gave him advice, and with a cap of invisibility, winged shoes, and a bag, he crept into Medusa's palace, looked at her reflection in his shield, and cut off her head with a sickle while she and her snakes were sleeping. Nasty! Two things sprouted from her spurting blood: Pegasus, the winged horse, and Chrysaor, the golden-bladed giant. The noise they made woke up Medusa's two monstrous sisters who chased Perseus, but he popped on his handy invisibility cap and snuck away. Perseus then put Medusa's head to good use – he went to a wedding party full of his enemies and turned everyone to stone (don't add him to your invitation list). Later he gave Medusa's severed head to Athena to decorate her shield. Athena wasn't done though. She returned to the palace to flay Medusa's skin and turn it into a breastplate that she wore for protection. I told you the Greek gods were weird.

Twisted sisters: The Gorgon sisters were, well, let's say "unique." There was, of course, snake-head Medusa. Her two sisters were Sthen and Eryale. Their heads were dotted with impenetrable dragon scales and their hair was also snakes. They were accessorized with great swine tusks, brazen claws, and golden wings. Oh, and they turned anyone to stone who beheld them. What a trio! No wonder they didn't have a social life.

Cool fact[1]: Medusa's blood can be used to raise the dead. If you take it from her right vein it heals and from her left vein it kills. So if you are doing a blood transfusion, choose carefully.

Cool fact[2]: More about her blood. From it sprang all the snakes that hiss and swish their way through Africa. So if you get bitten by a snake while on safari in Africa, you know who to blame!

The name game: *Medusa* means "cunning one," "sovereign female wisdom," and "queen."

High-school memories: She was the Senior Pin, the Prom Queen, and graduated with straight *A's*. Medusa (Meddie, to her friends) was invited to all the best parties and all the boys loved her. Basically, she put the *P* in popular and in party. But then, during one really great shindig, she suddenly stood on a pedestal and declared: "I'm hot, don't you think so? I'm hot! Hotter than Athena!" She was then voted "most likely to anger the gods."

Interview with the monster: "It's, like, so boring being a monster, I mean, once you turn all your enemies to stone that is. Then what do you do? You can't dance with a statue. No one visits anymore, they're so worried about being turned to stone. How selfish is that? And my sisters, well, they're catty loudmouths with no fashion sense. And my hair, it hisses. It's like I'm being followed around by an air leak. Stupid snakes. Stupid Athena."

Medusa, ugly or what? Though Medusa is often portrayed as one bad ugly sista, in many later artistic works she has the face of a beautiful woman marred by deep sorrow.

Medical note: Being turned to stone will cure your shyness. And your life.

What to do on a date with Medusa: Wear a blindfold. Don't ask to meet her sisters. Don't talk about bad hair days.

Hiss-torical origin: Snake-haired Medusa may have been a real queen who led the Libyans into battle against the Greeks. Perseus the Greek assassinated her. He thought she was so beautiful he cut off her head to take it back with him and show the rest of his army. This was before they had postcards or cameras, remember.

Loki

Occupation: Viking god, shape-shifter, trickster, lie-smith, stand-up comedian,

Nicknames: The Sly One, Trickster, Shape-Changer, Sky Traveler, Mr. Slapstick

Full name: Loki Laufeyiarson

Age: Immortal. He, like, doesn't age.

Birthplace: Jotunheim, a cold, unfriendly kingdom populated by frost and rock giants. Not a great tourist destination.

Fashion rating: *B+* Loki is handsome and fair of face, he looks good in his leather and loincloth, but the evil glint in his eye stops him from being a superstar hottie.

Loves: Making jokes, being sly, getting revenge, playing tricks on the gods and the giants, farting in public. Really, he thinks it's funny.

Hates: When the gods laugh at him, poisonous snakes, dwarves, being tied up with entrails

The lowdown on Loki: Ha! He's, like, so awesomely funny. He's the Norse god of mischief, which is kinda weird since Loki is the son of a giant and a giantess and technically not a god, but don't expect everything to make sense about Loki. He hangs out with his foster brother, Odin, the chief of the gods, and Thor, the Thunder god. You know him. He's the dumb guy with the big hammer. The mighty trio has oodles of fun traveling through the nine worlds, playing tricks on giants (which usually end with Thor crushing the giant's head), and teasing dwarves, elves, and mortal men. The gods all think Loki is totally hilarious – like the night he cut off Thor's wife's beautiful hair while she slept. Well, actually Thor didn't think it was funny, so Loki had to fix it by convincing two dwarves to spin her new hair from gold. Then there was that time he helped Thor get his hammer back from the giants by dressing the Thunder god up in a bridal veil and dress. Man, that would make a great movie!

Favorite insult: "Your wits are as blunt as your hammer."
Loki's children: Loki had lots of children, but that's because he had lots of affairs. With Angrboda, a giantess, he had Hel, a half-alive, half-dead monster-woman who ruled the world of the dead, Jormungand, a giant serpent that could wrap itself around the world, and finally Fenrir, a giant wolf. Gee, nice kids, Loki. He ran out of babysitters, since all of them were eaten by his children.

Shape-changing fun: Loki loves to change his shape. He once became a horse in order to trick a giant who was building the wall around Asgard. He has been a falcon and a pesky fly and a stinging flea. He has also been a giantess and an old woman. Oh, and a salmon. Which, he later said, was a fishy experience.

Loki's horsey tale: You see, once there was a builder who promised to build a wall around Asgard, the home of the gods. He said he'd have it done in six months and his fee was the sun, the moon, and Freyja, a beautiful goddess. The gods agreed. Then just before the wall was finished, Loki turned into a mare and lured the builder's workhorse away. The builder was furious. He threw off his disguise and revealed himself to be a rock giant. Loki's best buddy, Thor, shattered his skull for him. Loki came back later. Turns out he'd given birth to a horse with eight legs that he gave to Odin. It was called Sleipnir, and was the fastest horse ever. Now that's a weird story.

Invention he's been waiting an eternity for: The whoopee cushion

High-school memories: Loki sat at the back of the class and made everyone laugh by imitating his giantess teacher. She began crying so hard that she filled the room with salty water. Loki turned into a salmon and swam away. From then on the teacher caught and ate only salmon, hoping to devour Loki one day.

Tricksters and Treaters

A trickster in mythology and religion is a
god, goddess, spirit, or human who likes to
break rules, make jokes, steal, burp, and do
wickedly malicious things. Oh, and sometimes
teach lessons. They can be super-smart
(sometimes too smart for their own good) or as
dumb as a sack of pop stars. Tricksters include
Coyote, from First Nations' mythology,
who carries around a bag of songs and can
shape-change into anything. Or there's Eshu
from Yoruba mythology. (The Yoruba are an
ethnic group in Nigeria.) Eshu likes to wear
a hat that's red on one side and blue on the
other. After he walks through a village all the
villagers argue over the color of the hat. Then
Eshu comes back and shows them the truth – a
lesson that it's better to look at both sides of
a hat – or a problem. Something like that.

Interview with the trickster: "There are three types of humor: fart jokes, slapstick, and fart jokes. Did I mention how funny fart jokes are? Ha! Anything for a laugh, that's my motto. I still think the funniest thing I did was to get Thor to wear that dress. Man, he looked ridiculous. And his eyes burned like coals behind the wedding veil. Yep, the giants were surprised when he threw back his veil and started swinging his hammer. You could say they lost their heads. Ha! Oh, did I tell you the joke about the giant who farted and blew up his horse? Well, it wasn't a joke, it really happened. What a gas! Why am I so mischievous? I'm bored, bored, bored."

Favorite movies: *Dumb and Dumber, Blazing Saddles, Airplane*

The Giant

Occupation: Being big
Nicknames: Big Guy, Mr. Tall, Ogre, Tiny, Mr. Big Britches (Only one person called him Mr. Big Britches to his face – the giant ate him without even broiling him first.)
Age: 50 giant years (A giant year is one dog year plus two cow years minus a hen's age.)
Loves: Broiled boy on toast, golden eggs, the sound of a golden harp, bone bread, bags of gold
Hates: Bumping his head, Jack, falling from a great height, low-lying weather patterns
Fashion rating: C- Really, what's a giant to wear? Everything is too small and he dresses like a country hick. Overalls are so 1950s. You'd think with all that gold he could buy a nice suit. At least a vest.
Favorite saying: "Fee-fi-fo-fum, I smell the blood of an Englishman. Be he alive, or be he dead, I'll have his bones to grind my bread."
Home: A great big house above the clouds
Favorite Movies: *Attack of the 50 Foot Woman*, *King Kong*

A giant's tale: Like, once upon a time, Jack, a loser doofus, traded his cow for a handful of beans. Beans? Duh! Bad deal, doofus. His uptight mom freaked and threw the beans away. But hey, this is where it gets all weird, 'cause those beans were magic and they, like, sprouted straight up to the sky. Jack climbed the beanstalk and found a great big tall house. Inside was a giant woman who hid him in the oven, because her husband, Mr. Giant, liked to eat boys broiled on toast. Anyway, the giant came home shouting, "Fee-fi-fo-fum," and something about bones and bread. While he slept, snoring loud as thunder, Jack snuck out and stole a bag of the giant's gold and scurried home. He spent it all on video games and chips and soon climbed back to the house in the clouds, hiding in the oven again. While Mr. Giant was catching Z's (giants need a lot of sleep), Jack stole his goose that lays golden eggs. Cool goose, eh? Anyway, Jack, who was turning into a kleptomaniac, came back a third time and stole the golden harp that could talk, even though it was a harp. It cried out, "Master, master!" The giant chased Jack who slid down the beanstalk, grabbed his ax, and with two awesome chops, cut the stalk in two. The giant fell way far down and broke his crown, which is an old word for head. Jack became rich from the golden eggs and married a princess from one of those countries that still has princesses, and that's that. I guess the moral is, it's okay to steal from giants because they broil people, which is not really very nice.

Interview with the giant: "Jack? I'm so sick of being asked about Jack and his stupid beanstalk. If I'd caught that little Englishman I would've wrung his neck and used him as a toothpick. How would you like it if I snuck into your house, hid in your oven, and stole your treasure? Okay, so I probably can't sneak anywhere, but you know what I mean. Whenever I think of Jack, I just get soooo angry. Plus, I wonder what he'd taste like."

A Giant Collection of Giants

Giants are legendary humanoid creatures that are, well, giant-sized. They are sometimes called ogres. They are often amazingly strong, stupid, and violent. Oh, and they usually like to eat humans – broiled or with some mesquite barbecue sauce (apparently we go well with egg salad and chips).

Cyclopes: The one-eyed Cyclopes
in Greek mythology were
giants. They spent their time on
an island called Cyclopes.
(They were pretty simple.)
Odysseus, a Greek hero, got
trapped in a Cyclops' cave.
His name was Polyphemus,
but we'll call him Poly for short.

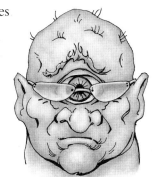

Poly chewed up several of Odysseus's crew. Odysseus then
got him drunk and stabbed him in the eye with a burning
spear. With Poly blind, the men escaped by tying themselves
to the undersides of his sheep. Poly felt only the tops of the
sheep to be sure the men weren't riding out of the cave.

Goliath: Goliath was a giant Philistine warrior in the Bible.
David was a young man who volunteered to fight him in a
match to the death. Goliath had armor, a shield, and a sword.
David had nada – except a sling. He slung a single stone that
knocked Goliath out. David then used Goliath's sword to
cut off the big guy's head. Can you imagine how many
people lost money on that fight?

Gog and Magog: The traditional guardians of the city of
London. They watch for trouble and do helpful deeds, like
lifting people out of the mire – an important job, since
there's a lot of mire in England.

Putana: A giant demoness in Hindu religion who attempted
to kill the infant Krishna by transforming herself into a wet
nurse and poisoning him with her milk. Instead, he sucked

away her life in an instant and she returned to her loathsome giant demoness form. Gross. Gross. Mega-gross.

A "real" giant: Robert Wadlow of Alton, Illinois, was born a normal size in 1918, but he grew to be 8 foot 11 inches and wore size 37 shoes. He worked as a spokesman for the International Shoe Company, which gave him free shoes. Everyone looked up to Robert. He was the tallest man in the world.

High-school memories:

The Giant was teased in school about his huge appetite: he could devour three broiled calves, an ox, a roasted teenager, and still have room for dessert. He had to pay double for his lunch service.

How to know if you're dating a giant: Look up. Way up.

How to tell if you're a giant: Look down. Way down. Is there an NBA sports agent holding a contract? Congrats, you're a giant.

How to deal with giants: Don't. If you are surrounded by ogres, the best thing to do is tell them jokes until the sun comes up. Apparently the sun often turns them to stone.

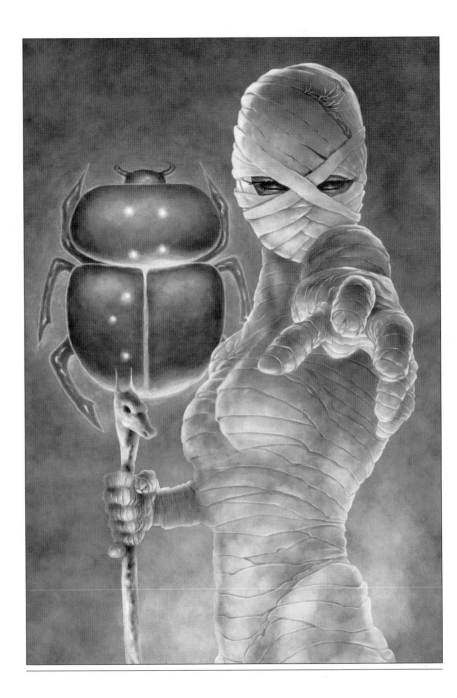

Tera

Full name: Tera, Queen of the Egypts, Daughter of Antef, Monarch of the North and the South, Daughter of the Sun, and Queen of the Diadems. Okay, like, what *isn't* she the queen of?

Nickname: Terrible Tera, Seven Fingers

Odd occupation: Mummy. Before that she was Queen of the Egypts, Daughter of Antef. . . . You know the rest.

Age: 4,500 years old, give or take a century. Doesn't look a day over 3,000, though.

Birthplace: Egypt

Feisty fingers: She has seven fingers on her right hand. Now let's say you want to give someone the finger, which one do you use? Her seven-fingered hand will hunt down and choke anyone who steals from her tomb. That is so cool! Don't you wish you had one of those for people who steal your lunch?

Fashion rating: *B-* She's always wrapped in white linen – but hey, she looks good in it.

Loves: Counting to 12, living forever, possessing other people, ruling over the Egypts
Hates: tomb-robbers, shopping for seven-fingered gloves, chafing from her bandages

Outrageous origin: Tera was created by good ol' Bram Stoker (as if he didn't cause enough nightmares with *Dracula*). She comes to life in *The Jewel of Seven Stars*, a novel about Malcolm Ross, a barrister (that's a fancy name for lawyer) who is infatuated with Margaret Trelawney, a prim and proper Victorian girl. In the middle of the night Malcolm is summoned to Margaret's house, because her father has been attacked and left in a trance. He has seven parallel cuts on his wrist. Who could have done it? A cat with seven claws? It turns out Mr. Trelawney is an Egyptologist who likes to bring his work home. In fact he brought the mummy of Tera back to his mansion along with all her jarred internal organs and the Jewel of Seven Stars. The spirit of Tera takes over Margaret, and the only way to stop the curse is to raise the mummy from the dead. (Just a tip: Raising a mummy from the dead never goes well.)

Favorite saying: "Hither the gods come not at any summons. The 'Nameless One' has insulted them and is forever alone. Go not nigh, lest their vengeance wither you away!" It's written outside her tomb. It's a long-winded way of saying, "Stay away from my mummy or I'll hunt you down and choke you with my seven-fingered hand."

Invention she's been waiting an eternity for: Deodorant that lasts 4,500 years.

High-school memories: Tera was the Queen of the Egypts, which meant that the teachers always gave her a passing grade. Otherwise, she'd have them thrown to the crocodiles.

Interview with the monster: "One day you're a queen, the next day you're a mummy waiting to be reborn and rule the world. The waiting is the hardest part. 4,500 years! Do you know how many times I've sung '99 Bottles of Pop on the Sarcophagus?' I hope my hair still looks good. Actually, I hope I still have hair."

Favorite movies: *Mummy of King Ramses*, *The Mummy*, *The Mummy's Hand*, *The Mummy's Tomb*, *The Mummy's Ghost*, *The Mummy's Curse*, *Abbott and Costello Meet the Mummy*

Cool fact[1]: Mummy is a weird word, ain't it? Well it actually comes from the Persian *mum* which means wax. Wax was one of the many things used to preserve a body as a mummy.

Cool fact[2]: The first "Curse of the Mummy" story is from Ancient Egypt. Setne Khamwas, a high priest, has the bright idea to steal the forbidden *Book of Thoth* from the tomb of

Prince Naneferkaptah. The prince's mummy rises up and
challenges him to a game of senet. Senet! That's like chal-
lenging someone to a game of checkers. Pretty dramatic!
Khamwas loses the game, but steals the magical book
anyway. Suddenly a bunch of really terrible and gross things
happen to him, so he breaks back into the tomb and returns
the book. Come to think of it, maybe this is the first "Curse
of the Overdue Library Book" story.

Why mummy, oh why? The Egyptians made mummies
because they believed the body was the home for the spirit,
and without your body you couldn't go to the afterworld. So
the body is kind of like a suitcase for the soul.

Places to find mummies: You can't swing a sickle without
hitting a mummy. They were found in Africa, Asia, Australia,
Egypt, China, South America, and many other places. Even a
couple of popes were mummified.

Extreme mummy makeover: Want to make a mummy?
First clean the body, pull out all the organs (except the
heart), dry them in natron (a salt) for 40 days, and embalm
them in canopic jars. Be careful, the intestines are slippery.
Be sure to use a hooked instrument to stir up the brain and
extract it through the nose. Soak the body in natron for 40
days and voilà! You have a completely dried up mummy.
Stuff the empty spaces with sawdust, put onions in the eyes,
and wrap the whole thing in linen, using your favorite
pattern. Then gather 20,000 of your closest friends and build
a pyramid.

Mummy's curse: "As for anybody who shall enter this tomb in his impurity: I shall ring his neck as a bird's." – *Curse on a mummy's tomb*

Ah, those pharaohs. They didn't want anyone in their mummy pits stealing their livers, so they came up with truly frightening curses. Legend has it that the tomb of King Tutankhamen (Tut for short) was cursed. A few months after the tomb was opened in 1922, Lord Carnarvon, who funded the expedition, died mysteriously. By 1929, 11 people connected to the discovery of the tomb had kicked off. Scary! Except Howard Carter, who discovered the tomb, lived to the ripe old age of 66. Oops. Curse missed him.

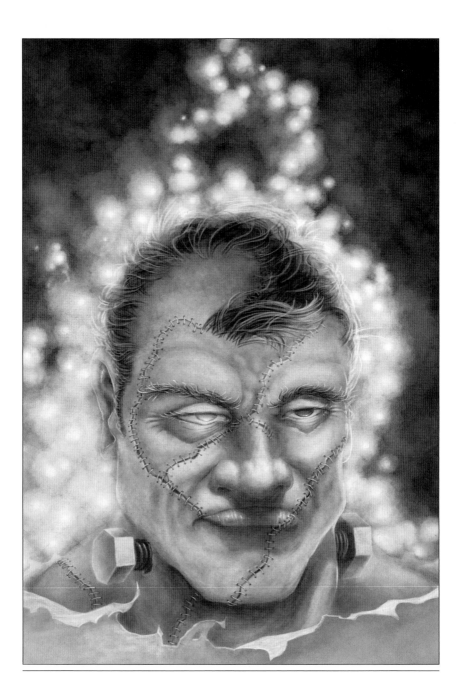

Frankenstein's Monster

Age: Body parts are various ages

Height: Eight feet tall, but too clumsy for basketball. Besides, he only eats the ball.

Birthplace: A lab at the University of Ingolstadt, Bavaria

Fashion rating: C- He's well-known for the ragamuffin look – rags, dark colors, big boots, oily hair. He's a bad dancer, and he's too big for a tux. His real saving grace fashion statement is his stylish stitches – though he is often mistaken for a hockey player.

Piercings: Two cool bolts that stick out of his neck. That's where he hangs his earphones, when he's not listening to Metallica.

Loves: Long walks in the icy mist and darkness, surprise visits to his creator, very tall women with stitches and bolts

Hates: Torches, angry villagers, when parts of his body fall off

Favorite saying: "Do unto others whatever you want, because you're eight feet tall."

Favorite movies: *Frankenstein, Bride of Frankenstein, Son of Frankenstein, Ghost of Frankenstein, Frankenstein Meets*

the *Wolfman*, *Abbot and Costello Meet Frankenstein*, *I was a Teenage Frankenstein*, *Young Frankenstein*

Monstrous origin: First things first, don't call him Frank, Frankie, or Frankenstein. He won't answer to any of those names. In fact, don't call him at all. He tends to kill everyone he comes in contact with. He is not Frankenstein, he is the creation of the scientist Victor Frankenstein. The "monster" or the "creature" first appeared in Mary Shelley's 1818 Gothic novel, *Frankenstein*. It tells the story of Victor Frankenstein, a dashing, dreaming scientist, who one day had the brilliant idea to stitch several hundred body parts together and animate them with life. The creature arose and Frankenstein freaked,

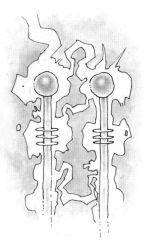

frightened by what he had created. The monster, its feelings hurt, disappeared. But he then did everything he could to get his creator's attention. He killed Frankenstein's younger brother, Frankenstein's best friend, and Frankenstein's bride. So Frankenstein chased the monster into the Arctic, and they both froze to death there. What a bummer!

Cool fact[1]: *Frankenstein* means "the stone of the Franks." The Franks were friendly barbarians who enjoyed meeting other people and conquering them. They "acquired" a Roman quarry in Germany in 500 AD and the name Frankenstein was born. Eight centuries later, Baron Von Frankenstein built a castle near the quarry. A few hundred years after that, Johann Konrad Dippel (Dippy to his friends) was born in the castle. He was a wandering scholar and alchemist who was rumored to know the secret to creating life, and he enjoyed making jigsaw puzzles with human body parts. Though the castle had crumbled by the time Mary Shelley came along, the stories about Dippel remained and may have influenced her creation of *Frankenstein*.

Cool fact[2]: Mary Shelley's novel was first inspired by a nightmare in which, "I saw the pale student of unhallowed arts kneeling beside the thing he had put together. I saw the hideous phantasm of a man stretched out, and then, on the working of some powerful engine, show signs of life, and stir with an uneasy, half-vital motion." Wow, Mary, that's some nightmare. Do you think it was caused by indigestion?

The most absolutely scary, and humongously frightening thing about Frankenstein's monster: He's a vegetarian. Who would have thunk it? All he eats is nuts and berries. He's a tree-hugging monster. Just don't get between him and his berries.

High-school memories: The only part of his body that went to high school was his big toe. Interestingly enough, the toe was attached to the field-goal kicker of the football team and was responsible for several game-winning field goals. It still aches sometimes.

Interview with the monster: "I have the heart of a thief, the brain of a murderer, the spleen of a sicko, and the hands of a psycho. Yet, I blame all my violence on video games. Do I have a chip on my shoulder? You bet. I'm sick of everyone pointing at me saying, 'Look at that guy. He's a freak! His head is enormous. His eyes are two different colors. He smells like a graveyard.' I especially dislike people asking me whether I have a body part from their uncle or cousin. Please. They're my body parts now."

The perfect birthday gift: A backscratcher long enough to scratch that itchy patch of dead skin in the middle of his back. **Medical note:** Though animating the dead sounds like fun, don't try it at home. First, it's a lot of icky work digging up graves and dismembering dead bodies. Second, if you actually can get your creature to come alive, there's a 99.9 percent chance that it will kill you. It's what's known as a lose/lose situation.

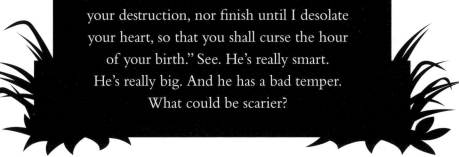

The Brainy Monster vs. the Dumb One:

Who's freakier, the movie monster or the monster in the book? In the movies Frankenstein's monster is invariably portrayed as a grumbling, mindless beast. But in the novel he is an eloquent, intelligent smarty-pants who knows how to read and understands philosophy and other big concepts. He talks all lofty, spewing out things like: "I will revenge my injuries: if I cannot inspire love, I will cause fear; and chiefly towards you my arch-enemy, because my creator, do I swear inextinguishable hatred." Or this: "Have a care: I will work at your destruction, nor finish until I desolate your heart, so that you shall curse the hour of your birth." See. He's really smart. He's really big. And he has a bad temper. What could be scarier?

Sasquatch

Age: Various
Height: Eight feet
Shoe size: Size 38
Weight: 750 pounds
Smell: Bad. Bigfoot is very much a smell-him-before-you-see-him type of creature. Eau de Sasquatch is described as a musty, pig-like, outhouse scent mixed with stale urine. No wonder they're often spotted alone.
Hairstyle: Most Sasquatches are quaffed in reddish-brown hair that surrounds their whole body – redheads are, of course, eternally cool. The occasional "punker" Sasquatch has white hair.
Habitat: The mountainous rainforest of Northern California, Ohio, Oregon, Washington, Idaho, British Columbia, and Alberta. He prefers to hang out near Walla Walla, Washington, because the name makes him giggle.
Fashion rating: B+ Although Sasquatch doesn't wear any clothes, he is quite fashionable – long, shaggy hair is back in style. If only he'd comb it. It's the sixties all over again without the weird psychedelic music.

Loves: Berries, leaving footprints, fish, rodents, starring in short films

Hates: Bigfoot hunters, when Yeti puts his feet on the table, baths

Favorite saying: "Hnnr hra Gaw." (Pass the berries or I'll rip out your spleen.)

Outrageous origin: The Algonquins spoke of *Windigo*, the cannibalistic monster that had once been human. The Lakota whispered about the *Chiye-tanka*, or the "elder big brother" who could race through the forest with the power and grace of a moose. Even Leif Erikson saw monsters that were ugly, hairy, and swarthy. Of course, he might have been looking in a mirror. In 1846, Mr. A.C. Anderson, a Hudson's Bay employee, wrote to his superiors about "the wild giants

of the mountains." In 1884, a train crew near Yale, British Columbia, reportedly captured a gorilla-like creature that was about four feet seven inches tall, with long black hair. "Jacko," as the creature was called, later escaped giving rise to many stories and legends, but not much in the way of substantiated facts. In the 20th century, sightings abounded. In 1924, Fred Beck and his comrades encountered the mountain gorillas of Mount St. Helens. They shot at one and were immediately attacked in their cabin by rock-heaving apes. The men escaped in the morning (apparently the apes got tired of heaving rocks). Suddenly Bigfoot tracks were discovered at worksites, fishing holes, and next to outhouses. The most famous sighting was by Roger Patterson and Robert Gimlin. In October 1967, armed with a rifle and a 16mm camera, the two explored Bluff Creek in Northern California and stumbled across a towering female Sasquatch who walked a short distance, looked calmly at them, then disappeared into the bush. Patterson caught it all on film and no one doubts the authenticity of the piece. Well, except for the people who think it was someone in an ape costume. There have now been more than 2,000 eyewitness reports of the giant primate.

Kissing Cousins (Blech).

The Yeti or Abominable Snowman is a relative of Sasquatch. In Tibetan, *Yeti* means "magical creature." He is shorter, with reddish-brown hair and has white patches on the chest. His long arms reach down to the knees, which is handy when his knees get itchy. He can be found in Mongolia, Tibet, Nepal, and Pakistan, though he seems to enjoy hanging around Mt. Everest and scaring climbers. Despite rumors, his personality is not abominable. It's his breath.

Giganto-what?: Some researchers suggest that Sasquatch is descended from *Gigantopithecus*, a giant ape that lived as recently as 500,000 years ago.

Cool fact[1]: The name "Sasquatch" comes from the Salish Indian tribe of British Columbia. It means "wild man of the woods."

Cool fact[2]: Another popular name for Sasquatch is "Bigfoot" which is of course a reference to the size of his feet. (Duh!) It became popular in the 1950s in media reports of giant-sized footprints.

Captured by Bigfoot: In 1924 Albert Ostman, a lumberjack, was camping above Toba Inlet, near Lund, British Columbia. One night he woke up bouncing – bouncing around inside his sleeping bag, that is. He was dragged over 20 miles and when the bag was finally opened, he was surrounded by four Sasquatches: Poppa Bigfoot, Momma Bigfoot, Boy Bigfoot, and Girl Bigfoot. Ostman was held prisoner in their camp for six days, listening to them chatter to each other. They did share some tasty roots and berries with him, though. It slowly dawned on him that he'd been captured as a husband for Girl Bigfoot who towered over him. Since he was turned off by women with underarm hair, he decided to escape. Ostman offered his snuff to Poppa Bigfoot who ate it all and turned red. In the ensuing chaos Ostman escaped. Worried that people wouldn't believe him, he didn't tell anyone about his capture for 30 years!

High-school memories: Only one Sasquatch has ever gone to school. He shaved most of his body, learned to say, "Hut one, hut two," and became the star of the football team. He is rumored to be in the NFL now, living in California. He can occasionally be seen on electric razor ads.

Beauty tips: The female Sasquatch uses a mixture of tree sap and fish guts to style her hair. It brings out the male Sasquatches from miles around.

What to do when you meet a real, live Sasquatch: First shout, "Oh my, I don't believe it. You're real! You're really real!" Then invite him to your next costume party. Won't all those Bigfoot skeptics you hang out with be surprised?

Interview with the monster: "My feet aren't big, at least not in comparison to my body. Everyone makes it sound like I'm an oddity, but where I come from, I'm as common as mud. And I don't smell. Humans smell. Tobacco, smog, deodorant – halfway across the forest I hear and smell you coming. Really, you're gross. And your feet are too small. And you're so hairless. Yuck!"

Loch Ness Monster

Nicknames: Nessie, ol' Ness

Age: Ancient. She could be hundreds of years old or millions, depending on who you talk to and how dizzy they are.

Length: 33-50 feet

Shoe size: Doesn't wear shoes

Weight: Nessie, like most girls, won't talk about her weight.

Birthplace: Loch Ness, in the north of Scotland

Fashion rating: B- She has curves with a capital C. Well, actually they're humps, but from a distance they look like curves.

Loves: Deep water, eating sheep, breaking the hooks off fishing lines, poking her head up whenever a camera is not around

Hates: People who say, "Here Nessie, here Nessie!" She eats them.

Distinguishing features: Two humps, a tail, a long body, a longer neck, and a petite head. Oh, and a gaping red mouth – she obviously wears too much lipstick.

Favorite saying: "Niseag gu brath!" Nessie's Celtic name is Niseag and sometimes Scottish people will raise their glasses high and shout, "Niseag gu brath!" Even though it sounds like swearing, it isn't. It's Gaelic for "Nessie forever!"

Favorite movie: *Das Boot, It Came From 20,000 Fathoms*

Romantic status: Nessie is single right now. Scooter, her high-school plesiosaurus sweetheart, was hit by a comet 15 million years ago. She still misses him, but she does have a BIG crush on Godzilla. The way he breathes fire makes her swoon.

Outrageous origin: Okay, the Loch Ness is like the largest body of fresh water in Britain — it's over a mile across, 24 miles long, and oh, about 150 fathoms deep. And it's murkier than the mind of a science teacher. You could hide the *Titanic* in there. Or a monster. The Picts, the original punk rockers who tattooed their entire bodies, left carved standing stones around Loch Ness that included depictions of a strange water beast. In 565 AD, Saint Columba was out

looking for something to do. (They didn't have golf yet.) He saw a large beast about to attack a man swimming in Loch Ness, so Columba made the sign of the cross and yelled, "Go no farther, nor touch the man! Go back!" The beast retreated. In modern times (if you can call 1930 modern), the sightings really picked up. Three fishermen saw a huge creature pass nearby – the wake rocked their boat and their minds. And they peed their pants. Okay, that's just a rumor. Then in 1933, Mr. and Mrs. Spicer, a local couple, saw a whalelike monster cross the road with a sheep in its jaws. Before you could say, "Whoa Nessie!" the press descended from around the world. A British circus offered a 20,000 pound reward for the capture of the beast. Footprints were found (they were hippo prints it turns out, from a hippo-foot ashtray) and pictures were taken – some proved to be obvious fakes. But the sightings continue. People from all walks of life – lawyers, priests, scientists, and even a Nobel Prize-winner have claimed to see Nessie.

Cold cryogenics theory: Cryogenics is when you cry because you come from bad genetic stock. Wait, that's not true. Cryogenics is actually when you freeze a body and hope to reanimate it in the future. So what might have happened is, plesiosaur eggs froze millions of years ago beneath the earth's crust. Then ten thousand years ago they unfroze under the Loch and the plesiosaurs have been living in Loch Ness ever since.

Really cool mutation theory: Newsflash! Disregard the other theories. Nessie is a mutated bottom feeder. Somehow a bottom-feeding fish, perhaps through background radiation (that's the stuff that comes out of your TV or your little brother's head), was mutated into a Ness-sized monster. So, Ness is either a fish or a mutated eel.

Really cool theory[1]: The Possible Plesiosaur Theory abounds. 60-70 million years ago a long-necked predator with flippers for feet loved munching on the flesh of squids and fish. Its fossilized remains look exactly like the Loch Ness Monster (if we knew exactly what she looked like, that is). Perhaps Nessie is a descendant of the plesiosaur.

Really cool theory[2]: Scrap that last theory! Nessie is a sturgeon. Not a surgeon, a *sturgeon*! It's a fish that can grow as long as 20 feet. That explains everything.

Really cool theory[101]: Stop the presses Nessie is a giant manatee!

Really cool theory[102]: No, a Zeuglodon (primitive whale, okay?)

Really cool theory[103]: Or a long-necked seal! A giant otter! Or a giant sea slug. Would you believe an eel?

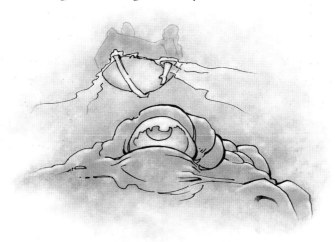

Not so cool theory: Maybe ol' Nessie is a hoax. Several of the photographs have been proven to be fakes. One was of a toy submarine with a plastic serpent attached. Eyewitnesses may have made up their stories because they were bored (it was the 1930s, after all).

Creepy cousins: Nessie has lots of cousins. In Ireland there's a peista in Lough Ree. A what? Where? A *peista* is a mere-monster. A *lough* is a lake. Boy these foreign countries can be confusing. In Iceland in Lagerfljót Lake there's a monster called Lagerfljótsskrímsli, but by the time you say its name it's disappeared. Other cousins include Brosnie in Lake Brosno, Russia, Ogopogo in Lake Okanagan, British Columbia, Champie in Lake Champlain, Quebec, and Issie in Lake Ikeda, Japan. Be careful where you swim.

High-school memories: Ness actually went to a plesiosaurus school in the bottom of the Atlantic. She was a straight-A student, and trained as a ninja. That's why she's so hard to catch.

Interview with the monster: "I didn't want to be a star. I'm just another lake monster. But one day I go out for a bite of sheep and the next thing I know, the lake is jammed with boats and submarines. I can't sleep because of all the sonar. I'm half blind from the flashes. And would you people stop throwing your old tires in the lake? Guess I'll wait another thousand years or so – maybe by then you'll all have died off and I'll be left in peace."

Zack

Occupation: Zombie

Age: 16

Height: 6 feet, 1 inch

Body parts: He still has most of his body parts, except his spleen, which he loaned out as a soccer ball. Another zombie ate it.

Birthplace: London, England

Fashion rating: G+ That's G as in gross. Zack hasn't changed his clothes in months, nor has he used deodorant or combed his hair. And perhaps worst of all, he hasn't brushed his teeth since that last brain-eating contest. (He won, consuming 23 brains in three minutes – though he accidentally ate one of his own fingers and nearly choked on it.)

Loves: Doing the funky-jerky walk, eating human flesh, playing catch – with human heads

Hates: Rigor mortis, when his prey gets away, people who are prejudiced against the living dead

Favorite saying: "Zroahhhhhhhhgggg – hooyah!"
Favorite movies: *The Astro-Zombies, Night of the Living Dead, Dawn of the Dead, Hard Rock Zombies, Night of the Zombies, I was a Teenage Zombie*

Outrageous origin: Zack is just one of thousands of zombies who lurch their way around planet Earth. One day he was minding his own business when a man-made virus escaped from a school lab and turned him and his classmates into flesh-eating, mindless zombies. And I do mean mindless – even when they ate their teachers, they didn't get any smarter. The idea of zombies draws its inspiration from voodoo. Movies, books, and video games have turned zombies into loveable, cute, undead creatures who crave living, human flesh.

Interview with the British zombie: "Right, so being a zombie is 'ard! You try always 'aving to 'old your arms straight out in front of you. It throws you off balance, right! And being undead ain't no blinking picnic. Me eyes are always drying up. Me tongue, too. Mummy still wants me to come 'ome before midnight! Midnight! All the other zombies get ta stay out, but not 'my little Zacko!' Mummy pulled me ear off last time I was late."

High-school memories: Zack had a pleasant experience in school, enjoyed reading and in fact was a teacher's pet. When he returned as a zombie he was saddened to discover those same teachers running in fear of him. Oddly enough, he was now a better football player.

Wacky ways to become a zombie: First, if a comet crashes into the earth, don't stand too close – you may breathe in dust from another world that turns you into a zombie. Same rule applies to a crashed satellite or meteorite. And don't poke around military virus factories or get caught up in biological warfare, all this could lead to zombie-itis. Radioactive material is also a no-no. Voodoo can be used to create zombies, but the major cause of zombie-ism is sitting too close to the TV.

Zombies' powers: Zombies are amazingly stupid, but very determined. Immediately after reanimation they are weak, but soon grow strong enough to tear you in two. They never sleep, so you have to be on guard all the time. They feel no pain and don't need to breathe. Oh, and their bite will turn you into a zombie within three days. If you're face to face with one zombie, relax – poke it with sticks and make fun of it – it's so slow it'll never catch you. Zombies are the most dangerous when there is a whole group of them. Are you stuck in a world populated by zombies? Good luck!

The clumsy zombie dance: Though the worldwide zombie threat is very serious, don't forget to pause and laugh once in awhile. See that zombie walk into a tree? Ha! That's slapstick comedy at its best.

How to know whether your best friend is a zombie: Is he wearing the same clothes he wore last week? Does he tend to lurch when he walks? Does he mumble or mutter a lot? Okay, everyone mumbles. Has he ever attempted to eat your brain? He's a zombie.

Voodoo, Bokors, and Haitian Zombies

The modern concept of zombies finds its origin in the voodoo faith, a tribal religion followed by African slaves in the West Indies. This new faith featured an animated corpse called a zombie. In Haiti, when you die, the family calls in the *houngan* (a voodoo priest) who brings along a live chicken, a pot, and several rattles. First he cooks up some chicken feathers along with hair and nail clippings from the body. Yum! Then he shakes his rattles, mutters incantations, and urges the *loa* (or soul) from the body into a bottle. He then gives it to a relative of the deceased for safekeeping. But if a *bokor* (sorcerer) gets his hands on it, he will use that bottle to raise the dead man and create a zombie, which he'll use as a slave working in cornfields or mowing the lawn – whatever task the bokor comes up with. Bokors also create zombies by poisoning someone with machineel fruit or datura, a thorn apple. (Don't eat thorn apples, okay?) When the person dies, the bokor calls him forth from the grave by whispering his name. ("Hey, doofus," won't work.) The zombie must reply, then he rises from the grave. That's why many people in Haiti are buried with their mouths full of dirt and their lips sewn shut.

How to kill a zombie: Zombies are already dead. You can't kill them.

How to un-animate a zombie: If you chop off their legs, they'll still drag themselves toward you. If you chop off their heads, they'll still try to bite you. All you have to do is knock out their brains and they'll stop.

Cool fact[1]: The Creole word *zombi* is apparently derived from Nzambi, a West African deity.

Cool fact[2]: A *coup padre* is a collection of herbs, human part, and animal parts that a bokor uses for zombification. He usually delivers it with a blow dart. So anytime you hear a *ssst* sound – duck!

How to deal with becoming a zombie: Relax. Life will be easy from now on. No more thinking, no more mathematics; just a good long game of Eat the Brains of the Living.

Baba Yaga

Occupation: Witch

Age: Whoa, is she ever old!

Height: Tall and skinny, even though she eats as many children as possible, at least two a week. It's part of her all-meat diet.

Nickname: She is known as Baba Yaga Boney Legs. (In Russian that's Baba Yaga Kostianaya Noga.) Don't call her that to her face, though. She'll bite your nose off. And eat the rest of you.

Weird body part: Her teeth are made of iron, which helps her consume children.

Other weird body part: Her nose is so long it touches the ceiling. Let's not even mention her nose hairs or snoring. Or the fact that her nose is blue.

Hairstyle: Wild, white, knotty, and windblown. Somehow it works.

Birthplace: Russia

Fashion rating: C+ Though her clothes are ragged, she does show us how those half-starved waif models will look when they're seniors.

Outrageous origin: Baba Yaga comes to us out of Russian folklore. Whenever she appears the wind blows wildly, the trees groan and creak, leaves swirl through the air, and a host of spirits shriek and wail. Now that's making an entrance! She zips across the ground on a mortar, pushing herself with a pestle, and covers her tracks with a broom. Oddly, she never uses the broom to fly, though she'll occasionally take to the air in her mortar. Her hut is deep in the forest and is built on top of giant chicken legs that constantly turn the house around. It will only stop with the right incantation and lower itself for Baba. When you arrive at her house she will ask, "Did you come of your own free will or were you sent?" If you were sent, she'll eat you, because all bad kids, if they're bad enough, will be sent to Baba Yaga.

Loves: Roasting, boiling, frying, basting, broiling, and barbecuing bad boys and girls

Hates: Chewing on tinfoil, heating up the pot only to have the child escape, when her house steps on her foot

Favorite saying: "You look good enough to eat."

Sleight of hand: Baba Yaga has some fine-fingered servants – three bodiless pairs of hands that do her bidding. They are rather handy to have around.

High-school memories: Baba was not popular in school. She was teased about her long skinny frame, big nose, and about living in a chicken-leg house. When she graduated she turned her class and her teachers into frogs then boiled them alive, cackling, "Who's ugly now? Come on, croak up."

Interview with the witch: "Listen, I'm not a bad witch. The Wicked Witch of the West, now there's a bad witch. Don't play Rumole with her, I almost lost an eye. And don't let her borrow your shoes. Anyway, I really don't do anything evil. I only eat bad children, you know, the ones who don't clean up their rooms, who forget to say please or thanks, or who whine all the time. It's a service for humanity."

Whither Come the Witches

Witches have been with us since the beginning of history, brewing up potions, ogling with an evil eye, square dancing with demons, and occasionally hanging out with teachers (though those are the *really* bad witches). The idea of witches comes from the sages, wisewomen, medicine men, and shamans of pre-historic times. By the Middle Ages, they were transmogrified into evil spell casters. All across Europe and in the New World women accused of being witches were burned at the stake, drowned, hanged, and worse. Nowadays witches are more popular, often appearing in sitcoms, movies, and TV shows. Gosh, some might even say they're hip.

Not so cool fact: In the old days, when people were dumber, the best way to besmirch a woman was to call her a witch. This happened in 1692 in Salem Village, Massachusetts. Two girls began having strange fits, so doctors figured they were bewitched. Upon hearing this, the girls accused several local women of being witches. Next thing you know, people were stringing up ropes and hanging witches left and right, imprisoning others, and generally putting the *hiss* in hysterical. By the time they were done, 14 women and five men were hanged, a beggar woman died in jail, and a man was, well, pressed to death while being questioned. More than 100 people were imprisoned. Turns out the girls were just having some heebie-jeebies after being told scary stories by their West Indian servant and had kinda made up the accusations. Oops.

Cool tools: No witch worth her weight in dried newts would forget her cool tools. Cauldrons are great for brewing up baby fat, snakes, bat blood, and toads. Brooms are used for flying, though in a pinch a shovel, forked stick, or a demon animal will work. And the stylishly pointed hat serves two purposes: to hold the hair while flying and to cut the wind.

Special powers: Witches cast spells such as Finn shot, which is a projectile in the form of a bullet or an insect that will make you sick or die suddenly. Witches can also summon whirlwinds (a handy way of messing up a party), or give you the evil eye – causing illness and extreme misfortune.

Familiar with familiars: Witches have *familiars* (that's *famulus* in Latin) – servant demons in the form of cats, bats, dogs, toads, and other creatures. They run errands, bring messages, help with rituals and spells, and fetch sticks. Well, just the dogs fetch sticks. Witches would even dress up their toads in black velvet, put bells on their toes, and make them dance. How entertaining! This was before TV, remember.

How to turn invisible and impress your friends: All you need to do is squeeze the sap out of a sow-thistle, mix it with toad spittle, and apply it all over your body. You'll turn invisible. You'll also smell swampy and get warts.

How to fly: First you need a pailful of toad excrement. Toad excrement! Never mind, take a plane.

How to know if you're dating a witch: She arrives on a broom and brings along a cauldron.

How to know if your teacher is a witch: Go right up to her and ask. If she answers, "No, I'm not," then she's obviously a witch. If she says, "Yes, I am," then she's a witch. If she turns you into a frog and boils you, you've proved your point.

Dr. Jekyll and Mr. Hyde

Names: Henry Jekyll and Edward Hyde
Age: Middle-aged or young
Appearance: He is tall and handsome or short, deformed, and ugly, depending on when you see him.
Hairstyle: Straight, perfectly combed Victorian 'do or a spiked mess
Birthplace: London, England
Fashion rating: B for Jekyll, who is a rich, snappy dresser, even though he is middle-aged. Ew! A- for Hyde. Hey, punk is in, especially Victorian punk.
Loves: Drinking potions, stepping on children, mood swings, raising cane, lowering cane, raising cane again
Hates: Mood swings, facial twitches, stepping on children
Favorite quote: "I knew myself, at the first breath of this new life, to be more wicked, tenfold more wicked, sold a slave to my original evil; and the thought, in that moment, braced and delighted me like wine." Okay, that's definitely wicked!
Favorite movies: *Dr. Jekyll and Mr. Hyde, Dr. Jekyll and Mr. Hyde: Done to a Frazzle, Miss Jekyll and Madame Hyde,*

73

Dr. Pyckle and Mr. Pryde, Dr. Jekyll's Hide, Dr. Jekyll and Sister Hyde

Outrageous origin: Okay, get this. In 1886, Robert Louis Stevenson, the author of *Treasure Island*, had a nightmare about a doctor who took a powder and turned into an evil, ugly man. So he sat down and wrote the novel in three days, calling it *The Strange Case of Dr. Jekyll and Mr. Hyde.* His wife, Fanny (don't make fun of her name – okay go ahead), read it and announced it was nothing more than a "shilling shocker." So Stevenson burned that book and wrote another version that went on to be a bestseller. It starts with ugly ol' Mr. Hyde trampling an eight-year-old girl in the street and laughing about it. A gentleman stops him and Hyde agrees to pay for the "trampling." The check he uses is from Doctor Jekyll, a well-respected doctor and millionaire (oh, and a master chemist, too). Next thing you know, Sir Danvers Carew, a popular old guy, is caned to death. Then a local doctor dies of shock because he saw Mr. Hyde turn into Dr. Jekyll. Jekyll locks himself in his lab, so his servant and a family friend chop down the door. They find Hyde's body. It turns out that Dr. Jekyll invented a potion that would split the soul into good and evil. Hyde is, of course, the good doctor's evil side. At first Dr. J.

just turned into Mr. Hyde for fun, but then he couldn't stop turning into him. That's bad news. They struggled against each other until they died.

Cool fact: Jekyll should be pronounced *Jee*-kill, according to the author.

High-school memories: Henry Jekyll was admired by everyone in his class and excelled at chemistry. Both handsome and rich, girls thought he was the ticket. But he did have a habit of going psycho and would suddenly become a burping, farting, swearing senior who would tease students about their braces. They had a saying for this: "Going Hyde."

Interview with the monster: *Dr. Jekyll*: "My lofty goal was to explore my darker side and to not be so, well, stiff in society functions. Socially awkward, I should say."

Mr. Hyde: "He means he wanted to learn how to party! Well, I put the *P* in party. I put the *P* in psycho, too. I also put the *P* in the punch (laughs loudly). Get it? Did I mention I put the *C* in caning and the *S* in swearing?"

Dr. Jekyll: "Anyway, it all got a tiny bit out of hand what with the trampling of the child and the murdering of the upstanding citizen. And worse: apparently there was even spitting in the street."

Mr. Hyde: "I put the *S* in spit, too. You name it, I did it. Dirty deeds done dirt cheap, that's me. The Master of Disaster. Woo-hoo! Bring it on!"

Dr. Jekyll: "You always have to have the last word."

Mr. Hyde: "No I don't."

Dr. Jekyll: "You do."

Mr. Hyde: "Okay, I do. What are you going to do about it? Bore me to death?"

Dr. Jekyll: "Bore you? I am not boring."

Mr. Hyde: "You put the *B* in boring, the *S* in snore, the *D* in dreary, the *D* in dull, the *T* in tedious, the . . ."

Freaky fog: In the 1880s, London was famous for its creepy, murder-hiding fog. Most of the fog was caused by the ubiquitous (that means everywhere) coal factories. Today we call it smog.

Jack or Jekyll? In 1888, two years after *Jekyll and Hyde* was released, Jack the Ripper began, well, ripping (and cutting, slicing, and dicing). His crimes horrified England and the world. He was never caught. It's almost as though the novel came to life. Shivers!

How to know you've become Jekyll and Hyde: You leave your bed unmade. There are several smashed beakers in your chemistry shop. People keep asking about your jerko twin brother.

Medical note: Changing into your evil, alter ego can be fun for awhile, but it is addictive. The permanent twitch you develop will also be bad for your social life.

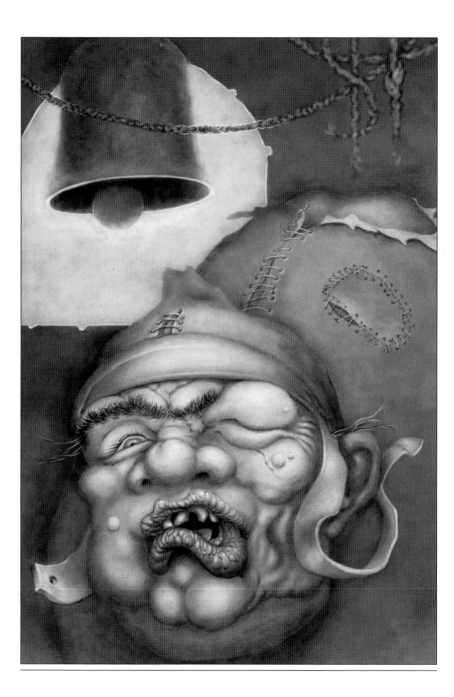

Quasimodo

Age: 19

Height: Hard to tell, he's always crouched over

Shoe size: Huge splay feet

Weight: About twice the weight of an average man

Nickname: Hunchback of Notre Dame, Quasimodo the One-Eyed, Quasimodo the Bandy-Legged

Birthplace: Not known, was abandoned in a canvas sack at the entrance of Notre Dame

Fashion rating: $A+$ Hey, one eye, a giant wart, horseshoe-shaped mouth, gapped-teeth, red bristly hair – he works what he's got. Everyone looks when he walks into a room. Now that's star power.

Loves: Ringing the bells of Notre Dame, Esmeralda, Esmeralda, Esmeralda

Hates: People who tease him, people in general, people

Favorite sayings: "Beauty is in the eye of the beholder," and, "Everyone is beautiful in the dark."

Favorite movies: *The Hunchback of Notre Dame, The Phantom of the Opera*

Outrageous origin: Okay, this is, like, a real downer of a story. Quasimodo is a character in Victor Hugo's *The Hunchback of Notre Dame* written in 1831. The novel starts in 1482 (let's just say a long time ago), in Paris. Quasimodo, a hunchbacked, deformed, hideously ugly guy with a grumpy streak and a good heart lives in Notre Dame de Paris, a sprawling Gothic cathedral. He rings the bells. He avoids contact with others, though he sometimes talks to Father Rollo, who adopted and raised him. Then one day, Quasi sees Esmeralda, a beautiful gypsy, dance outside the cathedral. He falls in love with her. So does Father Rollo, unfortunately. Rollo convinces Quasimodo to help him kidnap Esmeralda, but they are stopped by Captain Phoebus, who's this handsome cop type. Esmeralda thinks he's hot. Oddly enough, Captain Phoebus also thinks he's hot (he's extremely conceited). Later Quasimodo is flogged, and Esmeralda is the only one to offer him water while the onlookers taunt him. She then meets Captain Phoebus for some extra-curricular kissing and hugging. But Rollo stabs Phoebus and flees, and Esmeralda's accused of the crime. She is sentenced to hang by the neck until dead. Does Phoebus save her? No. Rollo? No. Quasimodo swoops down onto the scaffold and carries Esmeralda back to Notre Dame. How brave! How dashing! She's safe in the church, but when Quasimodo isn't looking Father Rollo tells Esmeralda she can either be his lover or she can hit the road. So she hits the road. Quasimodo runs around frantically until he finds her back on the scaffold. He arrives just in time to see the trapdoor open. No more Esmeralda. Quasimodo freaks, finds the priest, and hurls him from the cathedral tower. Then he weeps out of his one eye and flees. Many years later, in the vault where criminals are kept, officials find Quasimodo's skeleton with his arms wrapped around the bones of Esmeralda. I told you it was a downer. If you want a happy ending, watch the Disney movie.

Invention he's been waiting an eternity for: Plastic surgery

What to do if you're on a date with Quasimodo: Yell. He's deaf. Sadly, the ringing of the bells has done this to him.

High-school memories: In high school Quasimodo often sat in the back. He was voted most likely to hide in Notre Dame. He would ring the bells for lunch and recess.

Other Quasimodos

Quasimodo is everywhere! Open up a comic
book and there he is, fighting the Hulk in
Paris. Well actually, that was Quasimodo's
great-great-great grandson. Then there's the
Quasi-Motivational Destruct Organism
(Quasimodo for short) that battles the Fantastic
Four. And finally, there's Quasimodox,
a robot hunchback. A robot hunchback?
Wow! That's just stupid!

Interview with the monster: "Monster? You call me a
monster? I guess in your eyes I am. My mother abandoned
me. All shun me. All laugh at me. All point and say I am
hideous. So I hide in the dark shadows of Notre Dame. I
wait. I watch. I ring the bells. I bring beauty to your world.
And what do I get for this? I am tortured. And you say I am
the monster."

Cool fact[1]: Quasimodo is named for *Quasimodo Sunday*,
which is the first Sunday after Easter.

Cool fact[2]: *Quasimodo* means "half-made." Use this next
time you have an essay due: "I'd love to hand it in but it's
Quasimodo." At a restaurant try: "Whoa, dude, this pancake
is Quasimodo."

Cool fact[3]: *La Cathédrale Notre Dame de Paris* means "the Cathedral of Our Lady of Paris" It is usually just called Notre Dame for short.

Quasimodo – the coolest name ever: Yep, QM has the coolest name ever. It just rolls off the tongue. There's a band called Quasimodo, a song with the same name, a writer called Salvatore Quasimodo. (He won the Nobel Prize for Literature, of course.) The name just rocks.

Loba

Occupation: Werewolf
Age: 17
Height: Five foot seven inches
Feet: Two petite, nicely manicured feet, with hair combed to the side
Weight: Nice try. The last guy who asked Loba her weight found himself in pieces.
Smell: Eau de werewolf
Birthplace: Russia, Greece, Sweden, America, France
Fashion rating: B+ Slim, hairy legs and underarms – werewolves are oh, so European in style and panache.
Loves: Howling at the moon, stalking her dates, nibbling on ears, people who think werewolves aren't real (For some reason they taste better.)
Hates: Skinny boys, when bones gets stuck between her teeth, silver bullets
Favorite saying: "You are what you eat."
Favorite movies: *I Was a Teenage Werewolf, The Howling, The Legend of the Wolf Woman, The Wolf Man, La Loba, Ginger Snaps, My Mom's a Werewolf*

How she keeps her fabulous figure: Only eats whenever there's a full moon

Outrageous origin: In an unfinished survey of werewolves across the world (they ate the surveyor) over 25 percent of female werewolves are named Loba (she-wolf in Spanish, it's so hip). Our Loba is an amalgamation of all the other Lobas out there. All the way back to antiquity and beyond, people have been telling each other shape-changer stories. Since wolves have been mankind's most dreaded enemies, what could be more frightening than a human who turns into a wolf? The freaky ancient Greeks used to worship the almighty god Apollo Lycaeus (Wolfish Apollo), and told stories of King Lycaon, who tried to trick Zeus into eating human flesh. Zeus immediately turned Lycaon into a wolf, a shape he kept for the rest of his life. In the Middle Ages the sport of werewolf spotting became an international pastime – they were seen everywhere in Europe and a good number of people were burned at the stake, accused of being werewolves. Nearly every country has werewolf stories: in Canada they were sometimes called *wendigo*, in France they had the classy *loup-garou*, in Italy the manly *lupo manero*, Mexico the dreaded *nahaul*, and Spain the *hombre lobo*. It wasn't until modern times that Hollywood began making werewolf flicks, introducing silver bullets and raging hormones to the mix.

Interview with the monster: "People think BHMs (Big Hairy Monsters) like me are, well, snarly. But, really, I'm a cuddler at heart. I like to pick my prey . . . uh, I mean boyfriends, out of the crowd, hunt them down, corner them, and just cuddle them. It's so romantic. Cuddle. Cuddle. Nibble. Nibble. I just wish their heads wouldn't come off so easily."

High-school memories: Loba enjoyed high school, excelling at sports, especially running. She didn't do as well in cooking class, because she ate all her meat raw.

Wacky ways to become a werewolf:

Get bitten by a werewolf and live. Next thing you know, you're sprouting hair and fangs and going nocturnal. Or you could smell flowers. Really! The Lycanthropus flower (a white and yellow marsh flower), which grows in the Balcanic Peninsula will turn a human into a werewolf. Just pluck it and wear it after sunset when the moon is full. Then eat it. Before you can say, "Big Hairy Monster," you become one. If that doesn't work, go to a secluded hilltop during a full moon, draw a magic circle at midnight, build a fire, throw in some hemlock, opium, henbane, and parsley, then strip naked (don't do this in the winter). Smear your body with a werewolf ointment (often made with the blood of dead cats and bats – yum!), and put on a wolf-skin belt. Then wait. And wait. Soon a dark evil spirit will appear. Don't tease him about his horns. Politely ask him to turn you into a werewolf.

Wacky shape-shifter stories: One day in old Roman times, a guy named Lucius tried to use a stolen magic ointment to change shape, thinking he'd become a wolf or an owl. Instead, he turned into a donkey. Guess you could call him a weredonkey or a wereass. He's still braying about it.

Werewolf types: Alpha werewolves are those unlucky humans who have been cursed by a witch or bitten by a werewolf. They have no control over their changes and will become werewolves every full moon, prom night or not. Beta werewolves have either inherited shape-shifting skills from their parents, or use ointments or charms and can change at will. Don't make fun of their hairy eyebrows. They just snap, and suddenly they're snarling over their algebra books.

Werewolf powers: Glowing eyes, keen sense of smell (werewolves can locate their prey several miles away), long claws, razor-sharp teeth (the better to eat you with), night vision, ability to run on all fours

How to know whether your best friend is a werewolf: Does he eat meat? Raw? Does he have an excess covering of fur on his arms? Did he start shaving at age six? Does he have an extra-long left thumbnail? Eyebrows that meet?

How to kill a werewolf: Silver bullets, decapitation, a spear through the heart, atomic bomb

Famous werewolves: The wolf in *Little Red Riding Hood*, Wolfman, Wolfman Jack

The most famous historical werewolf: Peter Stubb was a gentle, soft-spoken man who lived near Cologne (apparently it's a sweet-smelling place). In 1589 he was tried for being a werewolf. On the rack he confessed to practicing black magic and to owning a magic belt that would turn him into a wolf. In that form he ate sheep, goats, lambs, men, women, and children. He was convicted and sentenced to having his skin torn off by red-hot pincers, then he was beheaded. Ah, the good ol' days, when the punishment was as gross as the crime.

Cool fact: *Lycanthrophobia* is a "fear of werewolves."

How to deal with excess hair growth: Find a strong gel for styling, and be considerate. Clean out the shower drain after every shower.

The Grim Reaper

Odd occupation: Gathering souls

Other names: Death, Thanatos, Anubis, Hel, Yama, Izanaminokami

Nickname: The Big *D*

Birthplace: That's the weird thing about Death, he was never born.

Fashion rating: *C-* Okay, who wants to make fun of Death's fashion sense? Anyone? Anyone? Fine, I'll risk it — a black robe? A scythe? A face that would make anyone scream? Please, could he be any more obvious? Death needs a makeover, ASAP. Start with a good foundation cream.

Loves: Gathering souls, arriving when you least expect him, hanging out with crows and vultures, Goth music

Hates: When he leaves his scythe at home, people who cheat death, always having to ride the pale horse

Outrageous origin: The Grim Reaper is, like, such a downer. If he comes to your party, just turn off the dance music and begin the weeping and moaning and gnashing of teeth. He never leaves without at least one soul. Sometimes he'll take three, or the whole party. Death personified has been with us since we first started thinking about – well, life and its inevitable end. He appears in countless myths and fictional stories. Our modern image of the Grim Reaper appears to be influenced by the black robe that was worn by priests or monks from the 15th century who attended the dying. The scythe is to remind us that Death reaps the souls of dead, and may also be a reference to Chronus, the Greek harvest god, who was also called Father Time. He, of course, carried a scythe.

Favorite saying: "*Tempus fugit* rocks!"

Invention he's been waiting an eternity for: A mechanical scythe

High-school memories: The Grim Reaper always hung back a bit from the regular crowd – he preferred to lurk in the background. People constantly looked over their shoulders at him, waiting for him to strike. He was never invited to any parties or other functions, but now and then he showed up anyway. Guess you could say Death was the ultimate party crasher.

Interview with the monster: "I'm so sick of people asking me for one more minute of life. Really! It's not my fault you don't plan better. Instead of watching TV, you could have been finishing up your life's work. But no, suddenly you want an extension. Well, life isn't homework. There are no extensions. Ever. Sorry that I sound so huffy on this point, but by Chronus, put a sock in it! *Hmmph.*"

Favorite movies: *Death Becomes Her, Meet Joe Black, Death Takes a Holiday, The Grim Reaper, Monty Python's The Meaning of Life, The Seventh Seal, Pale Rider*

Cool fact: In Mexico they celebrate *Dia de Muertos*, the Day of the Dead. One day you remember deceased infants and children. The next day you remember deceased adults. Not only can you buy special flowers and candles, but also candied skulls, coffins, and skeletons.

Cool superstition[1]: If you hear three knocks on your door and no one is there, that means someone in your house will die. Or else it's some kids playing nicky-nicky-nine-doors.

Cool superstition[2]: If you spill salt, throw a pinch over your shoulder to prevent death. Try not to hit your brother in the eye with it.

Cool superstition[3]: Never leave your shoes on the table or you will die by hanging. Sounds like something my mother used to say.

Death powers: He has no real amazing powers. Oh, other than taking your life away. Ain't that enough?

The Four Horsemen of the Apocalypse: Remember the Apocalypse? The end of the world and all that? Kind of depressing, eh? The thundering sound will be the four horsemen galloping around spreading havoc. The first three riders are War, Famine, and Pestilence. Death is the fourth horseman, riding a pale steed, sword in hand. Don't wave at him. You don't want his attention. Just go back into your bunker and wait until the thundering stops.

Death the taxi driver: A general rule of thumb is – don't bum a ride from Death. Turns out he has a part-time job running a ferry. We learn from Greek mythology that Charon, a grumpy ferryman, carries souls across the Lethe (River of Forgetfulness) to the Realm of the Dead. People pay him coins, which explains why some people are buried with pennies on their eyes. Death's other night job is driving the *death coach* – a black plumed coach pulled by a giant black horse. The faceless driver with burning eyes is good ol' Death himself. He goes to the house of those who have just died and knocks twice, then waits in his coach to give you a ride. Which brings up the question, how much do you tip Death?

What to do when you meet the Grim Reaper: Challenge him to a game. Chess, badminton, checkers, Monopoly – he's a sucker for games. Of course, he always wins, but at least you get a few extra minutes. Just be prepared for him to say, "Checkmate!"

Death Everywhere

It seems every religion has an image of Death. Depictions of Death were found in Anatolia dating back to the 7th millennium BC (about the same time your teachers were born). Death was pictured as gigantic black, vulture-like birds picking at headless human corpses. Stone Age cave paintings portrayed Death as a tall, thin, pale winged creature. In the Bible, the Angel of Death has twelve wings, has many eyes, and carries a sword. In Islamic literature, Azrael, the Angel of Death, has 70,000 feet and 4,000 wings and his whole body is covered with eyes. I guess you could say those angels are real "lookers."

Death popped up in Greek, Roman, Hindu, Mayan, and Egyptian mythology. Death can also be a woman, like Yuki-onna, the Japanese Goddess of Death who is nicknamed the Snow Queen. She uses her icy breath to leave her victims as corpses. Another deadly woman was Hel, from Old Norse Mythology – she was the goddess of the underworld and had the face and body of a living woman, but the thighs and legs of a corpse. Yes, her feet were stinky, but it's best not to think about that.